A
Feast
of Fun

9780602230715

D1792888

Acknowledgements

Grateful acknowledgement is made to the following for permission to use copyright material:

George Allen & Unwin (Publishers) Ltd for an extract from *Charlie and the Chocolate Factory* by Roald Dahl/J. M. Dent & Sons Ltd, London, for the first verse of "Adventures of Isabel" from *Many Long Years Ago* by Ogden Nash/McIntosh & Otis Inc. for "What's for Lunch, Charley?" by Margaret Hodges/Harcourt Brace Jovanovich Inc. for "Grandpa's Farm" adapted from *Grandpa's Farm: 4 Tall Tales in Story and Pictures* by James Flora, © 1965 by James Flora. Reproduced by permission of Harcourt Brace Jovanovich Inc./William Heinemann Ltd for "The Magic Pencil" by Charlotte Hough from *Charlotte Hough's Holiday Book*/Macmillan Company of London and Basingstoke for "Musician's Lament" by David Mowbray from *Poetry and Song* edited by James Gibson/A. P. Watt Ltd for the first verse of "Adventures of Isabel" from *Many Long Years Ago* by Ogden Nash for Braille and large print rights.

Every effort has been made to obtain permission for copyright material and the publishers would be grateful for any discrepancies to be notified.

Editorial consultants
James Britton/Diana Bentley/Fran Oliver/Pat Parsons/Betty Root/Anne Rogers

Level 9 artists
Willi Baum/Leon Baxter/Don Bolognese/Ed Emberley/Denver Gillen/Tony Heald/David Kelley/David McPhail/Tonia Noell/Jane Teiko Oka/Joan Paley/Arthur and Pauline Perry/Jerry Pinkney/Richard Powers/Ivan Ripley/Caroline Sharpe/Bill Shields/Lesley Smith/Mike Weymouth/Garth Williams/Hans Zander

© Ginn and Company Ltd 1979
Fourth impression 1981   158102
Reading 360 Level 9 Readers set ISBN 0 602 23071 3
Published by Ginn and Company Ltd
Elsinore House, Buckingham Street, Aylesbury, Bucks HP20 2NQ

Printed in Great Britain by Ebenezer Baylis & Son Ltd
The Trinity Press, Worcester, and London

Contents

Grandpa's Farm

Do you know my grandpa? He lives on a farm in North America. It's the first farm beyond Blue Beaver Pond. It has a big barn and a nice house. Horses and cows live in the barn, and Grandma and Grandpa live in the house.

"Years ago we didn't have any barn," Grandpa told me. "Then along came the Big Wind of '34. That's the wind that brought the big blue barn. But that's a long windy story. I'll tell it to you some other time."

"Now, Grandpa," I begged. "Please tell me now."

"Very well," Grandpa said. "I will."

The Big Wind of '34

"When Grandma and I first came to the farm, there was no barn — just a house. We were very poor and couldn't afford to build a barn. We had a cow, and she had to sleep outside. She didn't like that at all. On cold days she would get so angry that she wouldn't give us any milk.

"We tried to explain to the cow how sorry we were, but she wouldn't listen. When a cow gets really angry, she just won't listen to anyone.

"Then one day in 1934 the wind started to blow. Oh, my! How it blew! Harder and harder until it blew all the leaves off the trees. Stronger and stronger until it blew the trees away too. I had to tie down the cow or she would have been carried away. Even so, she sailed around in the sky like a big cow kite.

"I have never seen such a strong wind in my whole life. It made me so cross that I ran out of the house and threw a big chunk of wood at the wind. It must have hurt him. It must have made him stop and think how horrible he was being to Grandma and me, because the next thing, I saw a big blue barn sailing through the air. It swished over the house and settled there where you see it now. It was a good barn, but it didn't have any doors. So I shouted:

'HEY WIND! YOU FORGOT THE DOORS!'

"That old wind turned right round and blew back to wherever it had come from. In no time at all, I could hear him coming back. Sure enough, he had the doors for the barn. And he even found the pigeon house you see on top.

"When the wind had gone, I went out and looked around that lovely barn. It was just what I wanted. The only trouble was that it had settled on our cow's tail and broken it off. That made me very sad, but Grandma said not to worry. She said she had cow salve that would fix anything. But that's another story, which I will tell you some day."

"Tell me now, Grandpa," I begged. "Please tell me now."

"Very well," Grandpa said. "I'll tell you now."

Grandma's Cow Salve

"I have never seen such a fine salve as Grandma's cow salve. She rubbed some on the place where the cow's tail had broken off. The very next day the cow was growing a new tail. Grandma picked up the cut-off tail and rubbed some salve on it too.

"Do you know what happened? A new cow started to grow onto that old tail. In no time at all, we had two cows instead of one.

"Then Grandma rubbed some salve on all the tree stumps left after the big wind. New trees started to grow. That salve worked so well on trees that I thought I would put some on a cornstalk.

"WHOO-OO-SH! That cornstalk grew so fast that it knocked me over.

"Our pig, Wilfred, was chewing on an ear of corn,

and before he could open his jaws to let go, he was high in the air and going higher. He squealed with fright. I ran and got my axe. I tried to chop down that cornstalk, but I couldn't do it. It was growing so fast that I could never chop it twice in the same place.

"Up, up, and up it grew. Finally I couldn't hear poor Wilfred squeal any more. Wilfred must have stopped squealing and started eating because soon the cobs started to drop.

"All summer long Wilfred was up there eating corn

and dropping the cobs on our heads. Grandma and I had to put saucepans on our heads whenever we went out.

"When summer was over, the cornstalk stopped growing, and Wilfred climbed down. He had eaten so much that he weighed over five hundred kilograms. Biggest pig I ever saw. It's a good thing he did get fat. It's very cold high up there in the sky. He would have frozen stiff without all that fat to keep him warm.

"Of course, he froze stiff in that terrible winter of '36. Twice as much fat wouldn't have kept him warm that winter. But that's another story, which I will tell you some other time," Grandpa said.

I hope he hurries.

James Flora

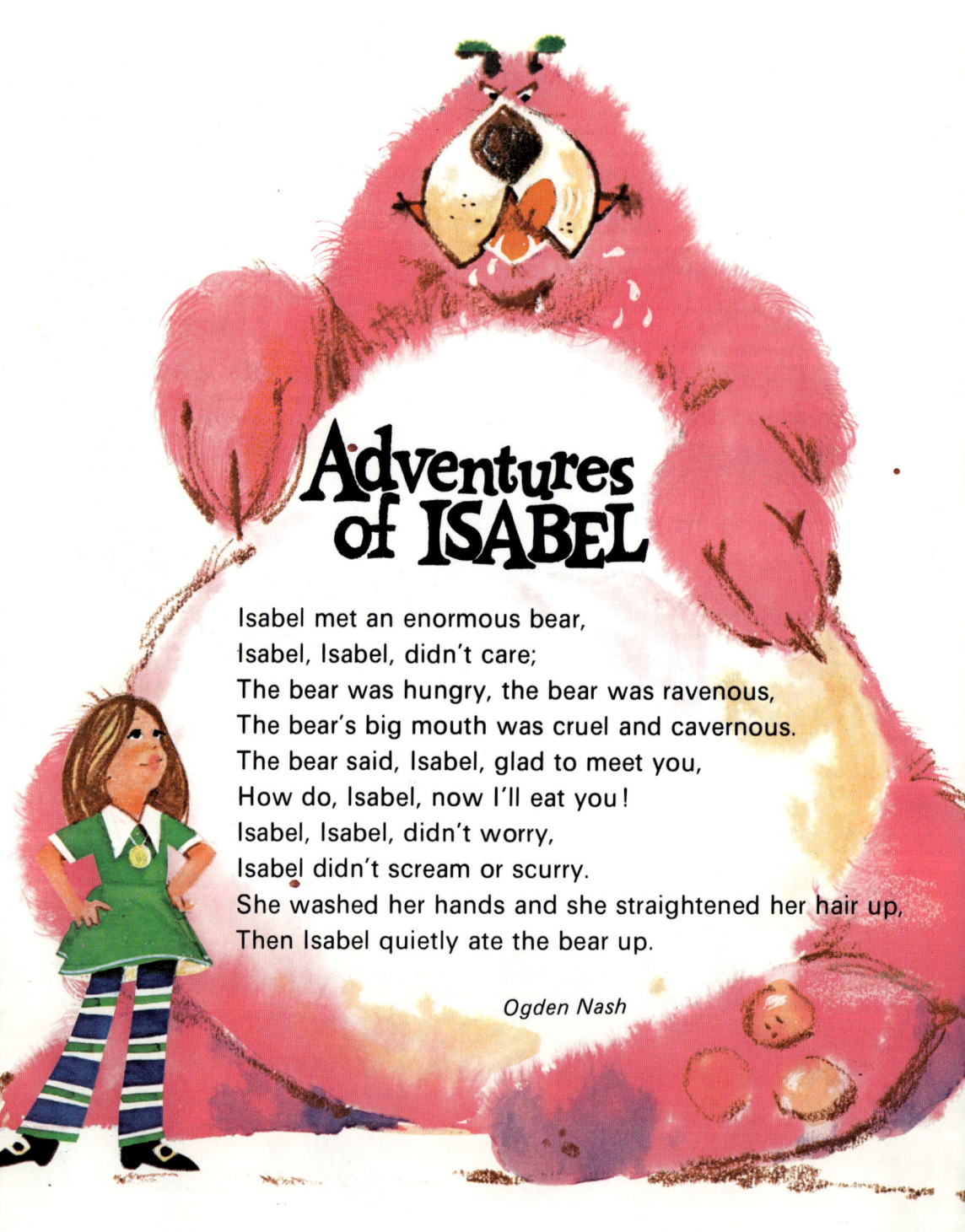

Adventures of ISABEL

Isabel met an enormous bear,
Isabel, Isabel, didn't care;
The bear was hungry, the bear was ravenous,
The bear's big mouth was cruel and cavernous.
The bear said, Isabel, glad to meet you,
How do, Isabel, now I'll eat you!
Isabel, Isabel, didn't worry,
Isabel didn't scream or scurry.
She washed her hands and she straightened her hair up,
Then Isabel quietly ate the bear up.

Ogden Nash

THE MAGIC PENCIL

One day when Annabel was throwing sticks for her dog in the woods near her home, she found a magic pencil in the undergrowth. She knew it was magic because when she drew a cat with it in her drawing book that evening, the drawing faded away and a dear little real tabby cat appeared instead and settled itself down on the mat in front of the fire. So Annabel drew a saucer of cream and that appeared too, and the little cat lapped it up.

It was nearly Christmas time, so Annabel went up to her bedroom and drew a fur coat for her mother and hid it so that it would be a secret.

Then she drew a car for her father and she looked out of the window and saw it come purring up to the front door all by itself. It was rather an old-fashioned one because that was the only kind Annabel knew how to draw, but it was beautifully black and shiny, with red leather seats and a big, rubber horn.

Then Annabel drew the car again, but hidden by trees this time, and she looked out of the window and watched while it started itself up and drove itself into the woods so that it should be a secret.

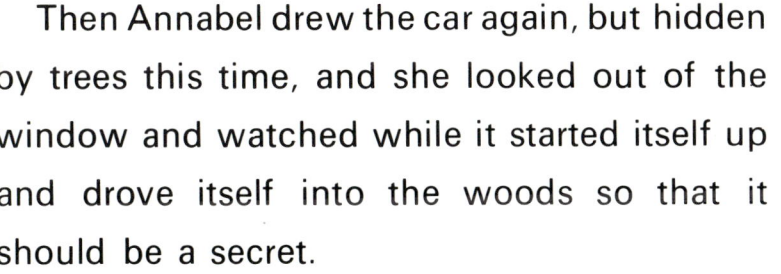

The next day after breakfast Annabel got very excited and she was just about to draw a lot more things when she heard her mother calling her from downstairs, asking her to take the dog out for a walk because it was a nice day and her mother thought it might cloud over later on.

So Annabel, who was a good child, put her drawing book away in a drawer and took the dog out for a walk in the woods.

When she reached the place where she had found the pencil, there was a goblin with a very worried look on his face, walking round and round looking for something.

As soon as Annabel saw him she guessed that he was looking for the magic pencil. But when the goblin asked her if she had seen it Annabel said, "No," but quickly added under her breath, "Not before yesterday," so that it would be almost true, but not so that the goblin could hear her.

The goblin looked so sad that Annabel felt very sorry for him, but all the same she couldn't bear to give it back to him before she had drawn some presents for herself. So she said she had to hurry and she called her dog and ran back home as quickly as she could.

She went up to her bedroom and drew herself a big box of chocolates and she ate nearly all of them. Then she drew a picture of herself with very thick eyelashes and long hair which came right down below her waist, and a beautiful party dress which was a long, grown-up one with a sash which tied in a bow. When she looked at herself in the mirror, she looked so pretty that she was very pleased with herself.

Then Annabel thought she would like to have a party to go with the party dress, and she thought what fun it would be to draw all the things she liked best at parties: crackers and prizes and cakes and biscuits and balloons and ice cream and sandwiches with flags sticking out of them to say what they were. But the more Annabel thought about these things the more she thought that she would do it in a little while but not yet, because she had just eaten so many chocolates. So she decided to go and call on her friend Jane and show her the dress and the eyelashes and the hair and perhaps let her do one little drawing for herself.

Jane lived in a house on the other side of the woods, and when Annabel came to the part where the goblin was, she looked the other way because it made her feel so bad to see him looking for his pencil.

But the goblin saw her and he called out, "That's a fine new party dress you're wearing."

"Yes," Annabel said, turning round, "my mother made it." And she added under her breath, "My breakfast, I mean," so as to make it almost true. But she went rather red.

But as soon as the goblin saw her face he could tell that her hair and her eyelashes were quite different from before and that she must have got hold of some magic because she was quite an ordinary little girl and he shouted out in a terrible voice: "YOU HAVE MY PENCIL!"

He started to run after her and Annabel
started to run away because she was frightened
of the goblin when he was so angry. But she
couldn't run fast because the dress was so long
it caught on the bushes, and her hair was so
long it caught in the branches, and she couldn't
see properly because she had so many eyelashes. Before long she fell flat on her face and
the magic pencil rolled out of her pocket and
the goblin pounced on it and picked it up. He
held it towards her and shouted:

"Magic pencil take away
The things she's drawn for herself today!"

Then the goblin ran off into the bushes
clutching his pencil and leaving Annabel sitting
there in her underwear, with her ordinary hair
and her ordinary eyelashes.

When she got home her mother was very angry with her for going out of doors in her underwear. When Annabel tried to explain about the goblin and the magic pencil her mother said she must have been dreaming, and when Annabel showed her the tabby kitten she said it must be a little stray cat who had come in through the window.

But Annabel knew that she hadn't been dreaming, because why should she have been feeling so sick if she hadn't just eaten nearly a whole box of chocolates?

But they will know, won't they, on Christmas Day!

Charlotte Hough

What's for Lunch, Charley?

Charley's Hard Life

"Hurry, Charley, hurry!" Charley's mother was calling him from the kitchen. She was packing his lunch box.

Charley Rivers always had to hurry to be on time for school. First he had to wake up, get up and wash. Then he had to dress and eat breakfast. In winter he had to put on his coat, cap, boots and gloves. And those gloves and boots were always hiding somewhere! Last of all he had to remember to take his schoolbooks and his homework — and his lunch box!

Somehow, Charley's lunch box was the hardest thing to remember every morning.

"Hurry, hurry, hurry. That's all I do every morning," said Charley, when he was eating his breakfast cereal and still hurrying.

"What's for lunch?" he asked his mother.

"The same as always," his mother said.

"Sandwiches, milk, fruit and cake."

"Again?" said Charley.

His father came into the kitchen to kiss Charley's mother goodbye.

"If you don't like it, go and eat at the King Charles," said Charley's father, looking at the lunch box.

Charley laughed. He thought his father was a very funny man. So did Charley's mother.

The King Charles was a big hotel that Charley passed every morning on his way to school. Mr Murphy stood in front of the King

Charles to open the door for people. It was a very grand hotel.

That was why Charley's family had a family joke. When the dishes had to be washed, or when you didn't like your dinner, someone was sure to say, "If you don't like it, go and eat at the King Charles." Then the whole family would laugh.

Start of a Bad Day

The next day started out all wrong for Charley. When the alarm clock rang, it was raining hard and a cold wind was blowing. That meant that his mother would want him to wear his gloves and boots again.

"Charley!" his mother called. "You're *awfully* late. I have got to go or I'll be late myself. Eat a good breakfast. Wear your gloves and boots. And don't forget your lunch box."

He had already passed the King Charles Hotel when Charley remembered that he had left his lunch at home. Well, it was much too late to go back now.

At lunchtime Miss Gray went into the staff room, and the children who were staying for lunch began to eat — everyone but Charley. He sat at his desk.

"Aren't you going to eat any lunch?" someone said. Charley looked up. It was Jane Lane.

"I forgot my lunch box," said Charley.

"You can have part of my peanut butter sandwich," Jane said.

"No thanks," said Charley. And suddenly he added, "I'm going out to lunch."

Now that he had said it, he had to do it. And there was only one place to go — the King Charles Hotel!

Lunch Like a King

The wind was still blowing hard, but it had stopped raining. Charley felt better than he had all morning.

Mr Murphy was standing in front of the main door of the King Charles. He was stamping his feet on the pavement to keep warm. "Well, young fellow," said Mr Murphy, "I don't often see you going by at this time of day."

"I forgot my lunch box," said Charley. "I'm having lunch at the King Charles."

"That's a good idea," said Mr Murphy. "Do you have any money with you?"

"I have some money," Charley said. He reached into his pocket and pulled out a note and a handful of coins. "I'm down to my last note. But my father said I could spend it if I ever really had to."

Mr Murphy looked at the money.

"Could I use it to buy some lunch?" asked Charley.

"I suppose you could," said Mr Murphy. "Go right in."

He opened the big front door for Charley. Then he led the way to a second door marked KING CHARLES DINING ROOM. He opened that door too, and Charley walked in.

The King Charles dining room was warm and smelled of good food. Grown-up people were sitting at the tables. Waitresses in blue dresses were moving around.

Charley had time to notice all this while he and Mr Murphy stood inside the doorway. Then he saw a lady coming towards them.

"This is my friend, Charley Rivers," said Mr Murphy. "He forgot his lunch box this morning and he's hungry."

He put his hand on Charley's shoulder. "This is Mrs Ruggles," he said. "She's the head waitress of the King Charles Dining Room. She will take care of you."

Mrs Ruggles pulled out a chair at a table by a big window, and Charley sat down. A waitress came to take his order.

"Soup," Charley said, "chicken leg, fruit salad and cake." Then he added, "Please." The waitress nodded and went away.

After a while she came back and put a cup of hot soup in front of him. She put a basket of rolls on the table and a butter plate with butter on it.

Charley drank all the soup. He ate a buttered roll. Then the waitress put a plate in front of him. The plate was filled with a chicken leg, some vegetables and gravy. On another plate at the side was a big fruit salad.

"When you're ready for the cake, just let me know," said the waitress. "My name's Nancy." She went away.

Charley finished the chicken leg and began to eat the fruit salad. But soon he stopped. He could not eat another bite. He was full to bursting. He saw Nancy coming.

"I can't finish this salad," Charley said.

"Oh, that's too bad," said Nancy. "What about your cake?"

Charley didn't even want to think about cake right now. He shook his head again. "I have to hurry," he said. "I'll be late for school."

"I'll tell you what," said Nancy. "I'll put the cake in a bag. You can take it along with you. I'll be right back. Here's your bill."

She put the bill face down on the table and went off towards the kitchen.

Charley turned the bill over and looked at it. He read what his lunch had cost — good heavens! All that for one lunch at the King Charles Hotel! Charley's stomach turned over.

At that moment Charley heard a surprised voice say, "Why, it's Charley! How did you get in here?"

Charley looked up and saw his father coming across the room with another man. They pulled up chairs and sat down at Charley's table.

His father said, "If this isn't King Charles himself, it looks like my son, Charley Rivers. Mr Rand and I are here to eat, but before we do, I want to find out what *you* are doing here."

"I forgot my lunch box," said Charley, and then he told his father everything that had happened.

"And so you came here," his father said. "What did you have to eat?"

Charley told him. "Here's the bill," he said. "I couldn't eat everything they gave me, and it cost a lot."

His father looked at the bill. "It did indeed," he said. "Well, I'll pay the bill, and you can pay me back. It will take you quite a while to earn the money. That will help you to remember two things. Don't run up big bills. And don't forget your lunch box."

He looked at his watch. "Hadn't you better hurry?" he asked.

"Yes," said Charley. "I don't want to be late. Goodbye, Mr Rand. See you tonight," he said to his father. "Thanks for paying the bill. You will have a nice waitress if you eat at this table. Her name's Nancy. Mrs Ruggles is the head waitress."

"You have made some new friends at the King Charles," his father said.

"It's my favourite hotel," said Charley.

Margaret Hodges

Musician's Lament

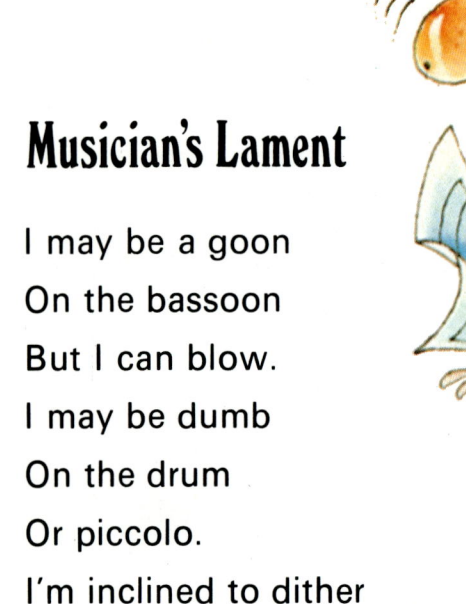

I may be a goon
On the bassoon
But I can blow.
I may be dumb
On the drum
Or piccolo.
I'm inclined to dither
On the zither
Or the flute.
When I sing
People fling
Fruit.

David Mowbray
(12 years)

Charlie and the Chocolate Factory

The Inventing Room
Everlasting Gobstoppers and Hair Toffee

When Mr Wonka shouted "Stop the boat!", the Oompa-Loompas jammed their oars into the river and backed water furiously. The boat stopped.

The Oompa-Loompas guided the boat alongside the red door. On the door it said, INVENTING ROOM – PRIVATE – KEEP OUT. Mr Wonka took a key from his pocket, leaned over the side of the boat and put the key in the keyhole.

"*This* is the most important room in the entire factory!" he said. "All my most secret

new inventions are cooking and simmering in here! Old Fickelgruber would give his front teeth to be allowed inside just for three minutes! So would Prodnose and Slugworth and all the other rotten chocolate makers! But now, listen to me! I want no messing about when you go in! No touching, no meddling and no tasting! Is that agreed?"

"Yes, yes!" the children cried. "We won't touch a thing!"

"Up to now," Mr Wonka said, "nobody else, not even an Oompa-Loompa, has ever been allowed in here!" He opened the door and stepped out of the boat into the room. The four children and their parents all scrambled after him.

"Don't touch!" shouted Mr Wonka. "And don't knock anything over!"

Charlie Bucket stared around the gigantic room in which he now found himself. The place was like a witch's kitchen! All about him black metal pots were boiling and bubbling on huge stoves, and kettles were hissing and pans were sizzling, and strange iron machines were clank-

ing and spluttering, and there were pipes running all over the ceiling and walls, and the whole place was filled with smoke and steam and delicious rich smells.

Mr Wonka himself had suddenly become even more excited than usual, and anyone could see that this was the room he loved best of all. He was hopping about among the saucepans and the machines like a child among his Christmas presents, not knowing which thing to look at first. He lifted the lid from a huge pot and took a sniff; then he rushed over and dipped a finger into a barrel of sticky yellow stuff and had a taste; then he skipped across to one of the machines and turned half a dozen knobs this way and that; then he peered anxiously through the glass door of a gigantic oven, rubbing his hands and cackling with delight at what he saw inside. Then he ran over to another machine, a small shiny affair that kept going *phut-phut-phut-phut-phut*, and every time it went *phut*, a large green marble dropped out of it into a basket on the floor. At least it looked like a marble.

"Everlasting Gobstoppers!" cried Mr Wonka proudly. "They're completely new! I am inventing them for children who are given very little pocket money. You can put an Everlasting Gobstopper in your mouth and you can suck it and suck it and suck it and suck it and suck it and it will *never* get any smaller!"

"It's like gum!" cried Violet Beauregarde.

"It is *not* like gum," Mr Wonka said. "Gum is for chewing, and if you tried chewing one of these Gobstoppers here you'd break your teeth off! And they *never* get any smaller! They *never* disappear! *NEVER!* At least I don't think they do. There's one of them being tested this very moment in the Testing Room next door. An Oompa-Loompa is sucking it. He's been sucking it for very nearly a year now without stopping, and it's still just as good as ever!

"Now, over here," Mr Wonka went on, skipping excitedly across the room to the opposite wall, "over here I am inventing a completely new line in toffees!" He stopped beside a large saucepan. The saucepan was full of a thick gooey purplish treacle, boiling and bubbling. By standing on his toes, little Charlie could just see inside it.

"That's Hair Toffee!" cried Mr Wonka. "You eat just one tiny bit of that, and in exactly half an hour a brand-new luscious thick silky beautiful crop of hair will start growing out all over the top of your head! And a moustache! And a beard!"

"A beard!" cried Veruca Salt. "Who wants a beard, for heaven's sake?"

"It would suit you very well," said Mr Wonka, "but unfortunately the mixture is not quite right yet. I've got it too strong. It works too well. I tried it on an Oompa-Loompa yesterday in the Testing Room and immediately a huge black beard started shooting out of his chin, and the beard grew so fast that soon it was trailing all

over the floor in a thick hairy carpet. It was growing faster than we could cut it! In the end we had to use a lawn mower to keep it in check! But I'll get the mixture right soon! And when I do, then there'll be no excuse any more for little boys and girls going about with bald heads!"

"But Mr Wonka," said Mike Teavee, "little boys and girls never *do* go about with . . ."

"Don't argue, my dear child, *please* don't argue!" cried Mr Wonka. "It's such a waste of precious time! Now, over *here*, if you will all step this way, I will show you something that I am terrifically proud of. Oh, do be careful! Don't knock anything over! Stand back!"

The Great Gum Machine

Mr Wonka led the party over to a gigantic machine that stood in the very centre of the Inventing Room. It was a mountain of gleaming metal that towered high above the children and their parents. Out of the very top of it there sprouted hundreds and hundreds of thin glass tubes, and the glass tubes all curled downwards and came together in a bunch and hung suspended over an enormous round tub as big as a bath.

"Here we go!" cried Mr Wonka, and he pressed three different buttons on the side of the machine. A second later, a mighty rumbling sound came from inside it, and the whole machine began to shake most frighteningly, and steam began hissing out of it all over, and then suddenly the watchers noticed that runny stuff was pouring down the insides of all the hundreds of little glass tubes and squirting out into the great tub below. And in every single tube the runny stuff was of a different colour, so that all the colours of the rainbow (and many others as well) came sloshing and splashing into the

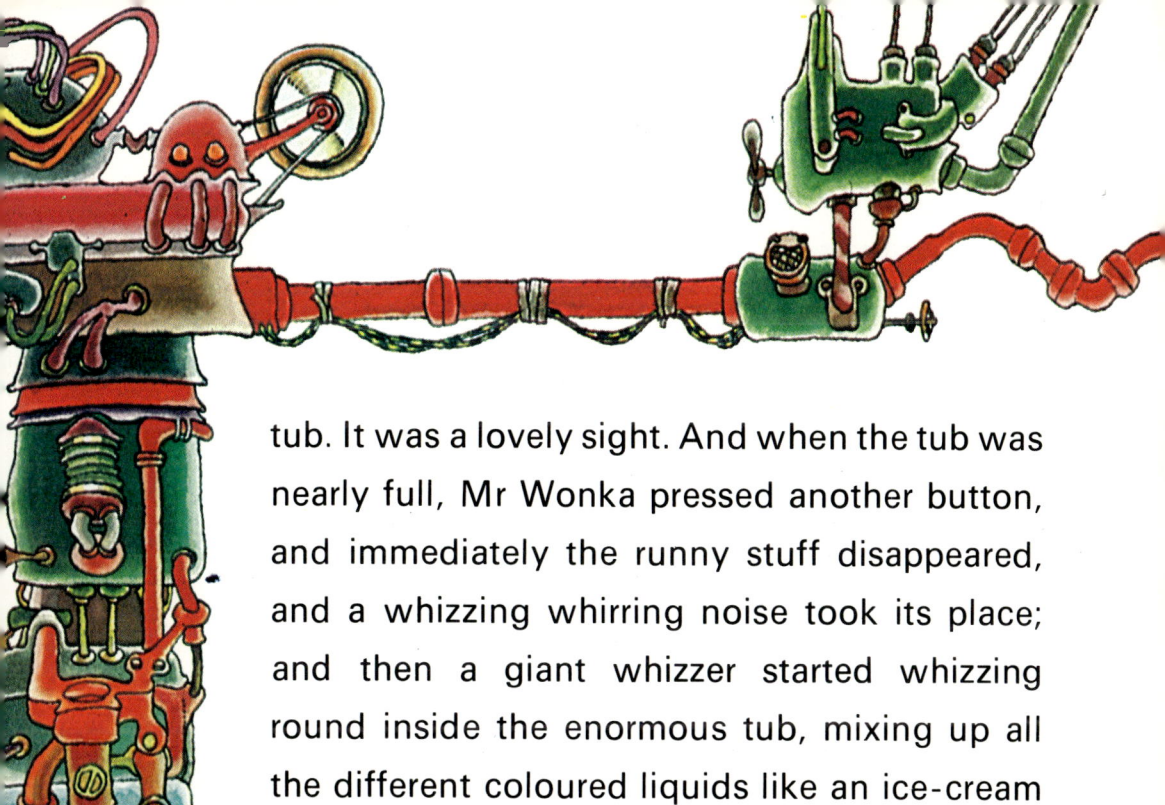

tub. It was a lovely sight. And when the tub was nearly full, Mr Wonka pressed another button, and immediately the runny stuff disappeared, and a whizzing whirring noise took its place; and then a giant whizzer started whizzing round inside the enormous tub, mixing up all the different coloured liquids like an ice-cream soda. Gradually, the mixture began to froth. It became frothier and frothier, and it turned from blue to white to green to brown to yellow, then back to blue again.

"Watch!" said Mr Wonka.

Click went the machine, and the whizzer stopped whizzing. And now there came a sort of sucking noise, and very quickly all the blue frothy mixture in the huge basin was sucked back into the stomach of the machine. There was a moment of silence. Then a few queer rumblings were heard. Then silence again.

Then suddenly, the machine let out a monstrous mighty groan, and at the same moment a tiny drawer (no bigger than the drawer in a slot machine) popped out of the side of the machine, and in the drawer there lay something so small and thin and grey that everyone thought it must be a mistake. The thing looked like a little strip of grey cardboard.

The children and their parents stared at the little grey strip lying in the drawer.

"You mean that's *all*?" said Mike Teavee, disgusted.

"That's all," answered Mr Wonka, gazing proudly at the result. "Don't you know what it is?"

There was a pause. Then suddenly, Violet Beauregarde, the silly gum-chewing girl, let out a yell of excitement. "By gum, it's *gum*!" she shrieked. "It's a stick of chewing-gum!"

"Right you are!" cried Mr Wonka, slapping Violet hard on the back. "It's a stick of gum! It's a stick of the most *amazing* and *fabulous* and *sensational* gum in the world!"

Roald Dahl

Glossary

affair   happening; event

anxious   worried; troubled

burst   to fly into pieces or break open suddenly

cackle   loud excited noise, usually made by hens

cob   *1* ear of maize   *2* small loaf of bread

disgust   strong feeling of dislike

entire   whole; complete

fancy   *1* to picture in the mind; to imagine   *2* to have a liking for   *3* not of the ordinary kind; arranged to please in some way

froth   mass of tiny white bubbles, usually on top of liquid

goblin   ugly, mischievous elf or fairy

grand   *1* large   *2* splendid

keep it in check   to control; to hold back

lap   *1* to drink by licking *2* top of seated person's thighs *3* once round race track   *4* to wrap over

line   *1* pen or pencil mark *2* cord; string   *3* occupation; business   *4* class of goods *5* to cover the inside

liquid   any substance that flows like water

luscious   delicious; sweet

meddle   to interfere with someone else's affairs

mixture   two or more things mixed together

note   *1* short letter   *2* musical sound or sign   *3* piece of paper money

pounce   to jump or swoop on suddenly and seize

precious   very valuable

salve   soft ointment used to heal or soothe a sore or wound

sash   *1* strip of ribbon or cloth worn round waist or over shoulder   *2* window that slides up and down

sensational   exciting; thrilling

simmer   to boil gently

sprout   to begin to grow and shoot

staff   *1* stick or pole   *2* group of people working together

suspend   *1* to hang from *2* to delay

swish to move with a light hissing or rustling sound

trail *1* mark or track left by something that has passed by *2* to draw along behind one

undergrowth small bushes and plants growing among trees in woods or forests

windy *1* having much wind; exposed to winds *2* containing or using many words; wordy